Zesty Delights

A Lemon Lover's Cookbook

While every precaution has been taken in the preparation of this book, the publisher assumes no responsibility for errors or omissions, or for damages resulting from the use of the information contained herein.

ZESTY DELIGHTS

First edition. January 5, 2024.

ISBN: 979-8224872138

Written by Jose Maria.

Table of Contents

Jose Maria

❖ Introduction

A. Brief History and Significance of Lemons in Culinary Traditions

Lemons have a rich history dating back to ancient times, believed to have originated in Southeast Asia. Traders and explorers spread this citrus gem across the globe, eventually reaching the Mediterranean. Lemons became prized for their vibrant flavor and versatility in various cuisines.

In culinary traditions, lemons have played a pivotal role, not only for their distinctive taste but also for their ability to enhance and balance other flavors. Their acidity adds brightness to dishes, making them a cherished ingredient in both sweet and savory recipes.

B. Overview of the Versatility of Lemons in Both Savory and Sweet Dishes

Lemons are renowned for their ability to elevate a wide array of dishes. In savory cuisine, their acidic profile cuts through richness, enhancing seafood, poultry, and salads. The zest and juice of lemons bring a refreshing twist to marinades, dressings, and sauces.

In the realm of sweets, lemons shine even brighter. Their zesty, citrusy notes can transform desserts into delightful, palate-cleansing experiences. From sorbets to cakes, lemons add a burst of flavor that captivates the senses.

C. Importance of the Lemon Tart in Dessert Culture

The lemon tart, a timeless classic, holds a special place in dessert culture. Its delicate balance of sweet and tart flavors, encased in a buttery crust, creates a dessert that is both sophisticated and comforting. The lemon tart has become an emblem of celebration, often gracing tables during special occasions and family gatherings.

This iconic dessert is not merely a treat for the taste buds but also a testament to the artistry of baking. Its allure lies in the simplicity of its ingredients, allowing the pure essence of lemons to take center stage.

As we delve into the world of lemon tarts, we embark on a journey that celebrates the magic of this citrus fruit in the realm of desserts.

Chapter (1) Essential Ingredients

A. Fresh Lemons: Choosing and Preparing the Perfect Citrus

Choosing Lemons:

When selecting lemons for your tart, look for ones that are firm, bright yellow, and free from blemishes. Heavier lemons tend to have more juice, a key factor in achieving a vibrant flavor.

Preparing Lemons:

Wash the lemons thoroughly to remove any wax or residue.

Zest the lemons before juicing to capture the fragrant oils from the peel.

Roll the lemons on a countertop to loosen the juice before cutting and juicing.

B. Pie Crust: Homemade vs. Store-Bought Options

Homemade Pie Crust:

Ingredients:

- **1 1/2 cups all-purpose flour**
- **1/2 cup unsalted butter, chilled and cubed**
- **1/4 cup granulated sugar**
- **Pinch of salt**
- **3-4 tablespoons ice water**

Instructions:

- In a food processor, combine flour, sugar, and salt.
- Add chilled butter and pulse until the mixture resembles coarse crumbs.
- Gradually add ice water, pulsing until the dough comes together.

- Refrigerate for at least 30 minutes before rolling out.

Store-Bought Options:

Quality store-bought pie crusts are convenient alternatives. Choose all-butter crusts for a rich flavor. Ensure the crust complements the tartness of the lemon filling.

C. Sweeteners: Sugar, Honey, or Alternative Options

Sugar:

Granulated sugar is a classic choice, offering sweetness without overpowering the tartness of the lemons. Adjust the quantity based on personal preference.

Honey:

For a nuanced sweetness, consider using honey. It adds depth to the flavor profile and pairs well with the citrusy notes of lemons.

Alternative Options:

Explore alternative sweeteners like maple syrup or agave nectar for unique flavor dimensions. Adjust quantities to maintain the desired sweetness.

D. Eggs and Dairy: Selecting Quality Ingredients for a Rich and Creamy Filling

Eggs:

Use fresh, high-quality eggs for a luscious filling. Eggs contribute to the tart's structure and richness.

Dairy:

Ingredients:

- **1/2 cup unsalted butter, melted**
- **1 cup heavy cream or half-and-half**
- **(Optional) 1/4 cup sour cream for added richness**

Instructions:

- Melt butter and let it cool slightly before incorporating into the filling.

- Choose high-fat dairy for a creamier texture. Sour cream adds a delightful tang.
- Selecting top-notch ingredients ensures the success of your lemon tart, elevating it from a simple dessert to a culinary masterpiece.

Chapter (2) Basic Lemon Tart Recipe

A. Step-by-Step Instructions for Preparing a Classic Lemon Tart

Crust Preparation:

Homemade Pie Crust:

Follow the instructions provided in Section II, B for making a homemade pie crust.

Roll out the chilled dough on a floured surface and carefully transfer it to a tart pan, pressing it gently into the corners.

Trim any excess dough and prick the bottom with a fork to prevent it from puffing up during baking.

Store-Bought Pie Crust:

If using a store-bought crust, follow the package instructions for pre-baking or prepare as needed.

Filling:

Preheat the oven to 350°F (175°C).

Lemon Filling:

In a bowl, whisk together eggs, sugar, lemon juice, lemon zest, and melted butter until smooth.

Assembly:

Pour the lemon filling into the prepared crust.

Baking:

Bake in the preheated oven for 25-30 minutes or until the edges are set, and the center is slightly jiggly.

Cooling:

Allow the tart to cool completely before refrigerating for at least 2 hours to set.

B. Tips for Achieving the Perfect Balance of Sweetness and Tartness

Taste Test:

Adjust the sugar quantity in the filling according to your taste preference. Some prefer a more tart flavor, while others enjoy a sweeter tart.

Lemon Zest:

The zest adds concentrated lemon flavor. Adjust the amount based on your preference, but be cautious not to overpower the sweetness.

Balancing Act:

Aim for a harmonious balance between sweetness and tartness. The tartness should be noticeable but not overwhelming.

C. Troubleshooting Common Issues in Tart Preparation

Crust Issues:

Soggy Crust:

Pre-bake the crust before adding the filling to prevent it from becoming soggy.

Cracked Crust:

If your crust cracks, patch it with extra dough before pouring in the filling.

Filling Issues:

Curdling:

Slowly incorporate melted butter into the filling while whisking to avoid curdling. If it occurs, strain the mixture before baking.

Overcooking:

Keep an eye on the tart to prevent overcooking, as it may result in a dry texture. The center should have a slight jiggle when done.

Undercooking:

If the edges are set but the center is too liquidy, continue baking and check at regular intervals.

By following these steps and tips, you'll master the art of creating a classic lemon tart with the perfect balance of sweetness and tartness. Troubleshooting common issues ensures a flawless and delicious result.

Chapter (3) Variations on the Classic Lemon Tart

A. Citrus Medley Tart: Incorporating a Mix of Citrus Fruits for a Vibrant Twist

Ingredients:

- 1 classic lemon tart (prepared as per Section III)
- Assorted citrus fruits (oranges, grapefruits, blood oranges)
- 1/4 cup citrus marmalade or orange blossom honey for glaze

Instructions:

Prepare the Classic Lemon Tart:

Follow the basic lemon tart recipe outlined in Section III.

Citrus Medley Topping:

Thinly slice assorted citrus fruits and arrange them in an overlapping pattern on top of the cooled lemon tart.

Glaze:

Warm the citrus marmalade or orange blossom honey and brush it over the citrus slices for a glossy finish.

Chill and Serve:

Chill the tart for an additional hour to set the glaze before serving. Enjoy the burst of citrus flavors in every bite!

B. Lavender Lemon Tart: Infusing Floral Notes for a Unique Flavor Profile

Ingredients:

- 1 classic lemon tart (prepared as per Section III)
- 1 tablespoon dried culinary lavender
- Lavender-infused honey for drizzling (optional)

Instructions:

Prepare the Classic Lemon Tart:

Follow the basic lemon tart recipe outlined in Section III.

Lavender Infusion:

In a small saucepan, gently heat the dried lavender with a 1/4 cup of water. Let it simmer for 5 minutes, then strain to extract the lavender-infused water.

Lavender Lemon Filling:

Add 1-2 tablespoons of the lavender-infused water to the lemon filling for a subtle floral note.

Baking and Drizzling:

Bake the tart as directed. Optionally, drizzle lavender-infused honey over the cooled tart before serving.

Chill and Enjoy:

Chill the tart for at least 2 hours to allow the flavors to meld. Delight in the unique combination of citrus and floral notes.

C. Toasted Coconut Lemon Tart: Adding a Tropical Touch to the Traditional Recipe

Ingredients:

- **1 classic lemon tart (prepared as per Section III)**
- **1/2 cup shredded coconut, toasted**
- **Whipped coconut cream for serving**

Instructions:

Prepare the Classic Lemon Tart:

Follow the basic lemon tart recipe outlined in Section III.

Toasting Coconut:

In a dry skillet over medium heat, toast the shredded coconut until golden brown. Keep an eye on it, as it can burn quickly.

Coconut Lemon Filling:

Sprinkle the toasted coconut over the lemon filling before baking, pressing it gently into the surface.

Baking and Serving:

Bake the tart as directed. Once cooled, serve each slice with a dollop of whipped coconut cream.

Chill and Indulge:

Chill the tart to allow the flavors to meld. Enjoy the tropical twist with the delightful crunch of toasted coconut.

These variations on the classic lemon tart offer a spectrum of flavors, from the vibrant citrus medley to the delicate lavender infusion and the tropical allure of toasted coconut. Choose the one that suits your taste or experiment with all three for a diverse dessert experience.

Chapter (4) Gluten-Free and Vegan Options

A. Almond Flour Crust and Alternative Flours for a Gluten-Free Version

Gluten-Free Almond Flour Crust:

Ingredients:

- **1 1/2 cups almond flour**
- **1/4 cup coconut flour**
- **1/4 cup melted coconut oil or dairy-free butter**
- **2 tablespoons maple syrup or agave nectar**
- **Pinch of salt**

Instructions:

- Preheat the oven to 350°F (175°C).
- In a bowl, combine almond flour, coconut flour, melted coconut oil, maple syrup, and a pinch of salt.
- Press the mixture into a tart pan, forming an even crust.
- Bake for 10-12 minutes or until the crust is golden brown.
- Allow it to cool completely before adding the lemon filling.

B. Dairy-Free and Egg-Free Alternatives for a Vegan-Friendly Option

Vegan Lemon Tart Filling:

Ingredients:

- 1 cup full-fat coconut milk
- 1 cup cashews, soaked for 4 hours or overnight
- 1/2 cup maple syrup
- 1/2 cup lemon juice
- Zest of 2 lemons
- 1/4 cup melted coconut oil
- 1 teaspoon vanilla extract

Instructions:

- Blend soaked cashews and coconut milk until smooth.
- Add maple syrup, lemon juice, lemon zest, melted coconut oil, and vanilla extract. Blend until well combined.
- Pour the vegan lemon filling into the pre-baked almond flour crust.
- Bake for 25-30 minutes at 350°F (175°C) or until the edges are set.

C. Tips for Adapting the Recipe to Various Dietary Preferences

Flour Alternatives:

Experiment with other gluten-free flours like rice flour or a gluten-free flour blend for the crust.

For nut-free options, consider using oat flour or a blend of gluten-free flours.

Sweeteners:

Swap out traditional sugar for coconut sugar, date sugar, or other preferred natural sweeteners.

Adjust quantities based on the sweetness level desired.

Egg Replacements:

In non-vegan versions, try using flax eggs (1 tablespoon ground flaxseed + 3 tablespoons water per egg) or applesauce as egg replacements.

Dairy Alternatives:

Use plant-based butters or margarine for the crust.

Experiment with almond, soy, or oat milk as a substitute for dairy in the filling.

Taste and Adjust:

Taste the filling before baking and adjust sweetness or tartness according to preference.

Texture Modifications:

To achieve a creamier texture in vegan versions, consider adding coconut cream or silken tofu to the filling.

By adapting the recipe to different dietary preferences, you can cater to a broader audience while maintaining the delightful essence of a lemon tart. Feel free to get creative and explore a variety of ingredients to suit individual tastes and needs.

Chapter (5) Garnishes and Presentation

A. Whipped Cream, Berries, and Mint: Enhancing the Visual Appeal

Whipped Cream and Berry Topping:

Ingredients:

- 1 cup heavy cream or coconut cream (for a vegan option)
- 2 tablespoons powdered sugar
- Mixed berries (strawberries, blueberries, raspberries)
- Fresh mint leaves for garnish

Instructions:

- In a chilled bowl, whip the cream until soft peaks form. If using coconut cream, ensure it's well chilled for a creamy consistency.
- Sweeten the whipped cream with powdered sugar to taste.
- Spoon dollops of whipped cream onto individual slices of lemon tart.
- Garnish with a vibrant assortment of mixed berries.
- Place fresh mint leaves delicately on top for a burst of color and aroma.

B. Creative Plating Ideas for Special Occasions

Individual Tartlets:

Create mini lemon tartlets for an elegant and personal touch during events or gatherings.

Arrange them on a tiered serving platter for a visually appealing display.

Edible Flowers:

Garnish with edible flowers like pansies or violets for a sophisticated and artistic presentation.

Chocolate Drizzle:

Drizzle melted dark chocolate over the lemon tart slices for a decadent twist.

Use a piping bag to create intricate chocolate patterns.

Lemon Zest Designs:

Use extra lemon zest to create patterns or write personalized messages on the tart's surface.

C. Serving Suggestions and Accompaniments

Tea Pairing:

Serve slices of lemon tart with a side of Earl Grey or chamomile tea for a delightful afternoon treat.

Ice Cream Complement:

Accompany each slice with a scoop of vanilla or coconut milk ice cream for a contrasting texture and temperature.

Lemon Curd Drizzle:

Drizzle a small amount of homemade lemon curd over the tart just before serving for an extra burst of citrus flavor.

Caramelized Citrus Slices:

Garnish with caramelized lemon or orange slices for an added layer of sweetness and sophistication.

Nuts and Seeds:

Sprinkle chopped pistachios, almonds, or sesame seeds over the whipped cream for a crunchy element.

Consider the occasion and your guests' preferences when choosing garnishes and plating ideas. The goal is to enhance the overall experience, making each serving a feast for the eyes as well as the taste buds.

Chapter (6) Lemon-Inspired Beverages

A. Lemonade and Citrus-Infused Drinks

Classic Lemonade:

Ingredients:

- 1 cup fresh lemon juice
- 1 cup granulated sugar
- 6 cups cold water
- Lemon slices for garnish
- Fresh mint leaves for garnish

Instructions:

- In a pitcher, combine fresh lemon juice and granulated sugar. Stir until the sugar dissolves.
- Add cold water and mix well.
- Refrigerate for at least an hour to chill.
- Serve over ice, garnished with lemon slices and fresh mint.

Citrus Sparkler:

Ingredients:

- 1 cup mixed citrus juice (lemon, orange, grapefruit)
- 2 tablespoons honey or agave syrup
- Sparkling water
- Ice cubes
- Citrus slices for garnish

Instructions:

- In a glass, combine mixed citrus juice and honey/agave.
- Add ice cubes and top with sparkling water.
- Stir gently and garnish with citrus slices.

B. Lemon-Flavored Cocktails for a Refreshing Pairing
Lemon Basil Mojito:
Ingredients:

- **2 oz white rum**
- **1 oz fresh lemon juice**
- **1 oz simple syrup**
- **Handful of fresh basil leaves**
- **Club soda**
- **Ice cubes**
- **Lemon wheel for garnish**

Instructions:

- In a glass, muddle basil leaves with fresh lemon juice and simple syrup.
- Add white rum and ice cubes, then top with club soda.
- Stir gently and garnish with a lemon wheel.

Limoncello Spritz:

Ingredients:

- **2 oz limoncello liqueur**
- **4 oz prosecco**
- **Splash of club soda**
- **Ice cubes**
- **Lemon twist for garnish**

Instructions:

- Fill a glass with ice cubes.
- Pour limoncello over the ice, followed by prosecco and a splash of club soda.
- Stir gently and garnish with a lemon twist.

C. Tea and Dessert Pairing Recommendations

Earl Grey Tea:

Pairing:

The bergamot in Earl Grey complements the citrusy notes in the lemon tart.

Serve hot or as an iced tea for a refreshing contrast.

Chamomile Tea:

Pairing:

Chamomile's floral undertones create a soothing balance with the tartness of the lemon tart.

Serve warm with a slice of lemon tart for a calming dessert experience.

Green Tea:

Pairing:

Green tea's grassy notes provide a subtle backdrop to the vibrant flavors of the lemon tart.

Brew a light green tea and serve alongside the tart.

Experiment with different beverage pairings to find the combination that best suits your taste preferences and the occasion. Whether you prefer a non-alcoholic refreshment or a spirited cocktail, the lemon-inspired beverages will complement the zesty delights of your lemon tart.

Chapter (7) Tips for Storing and Freezing

A. Proper Storage Techniques to Maintain Freshness

Short-Term Storage (Up to 2 Days):

Refrigeration:

Store the lemon tart in an airtight container in the refrigerator.

If the tart is topped with whipped cream or fresh berries, cover it loosely with plastic wrap to prevent them from becoming too moist.

Avoid Odor Contamination:

Keep the lemon tart away from strong-smelling foods in the refrigerator to prevent flavor transfer.

Long-Term Storage (More than 2 Days):

Freezing:

For longer storage, freeze the lemon tart without toppings.

Wrap the entire tart or individual slices tightly in plastic wrap, followed by a layer of aluminum foil.

Freezer-Friendly Toppings:

If applicable, freeze whipped cream separately in a sealed container, and add fresh berries or mint after thawing.

B. Freezing Guidelines for Make-Ahead Convenience

Freezing the Entire Tart:

Wrap:

Allow the lemon tart to cool completely.

Wrap the tart securely in plastic wrap, ensuring it's well covered to prevent freezer burn.

Aluminum Foil:

Add an additional layer of aluminum foil around the wrapped tart for extra protection.

Label and Date:

Label the package with the date of preparation for easy tracking.

Freeze:

Place the wrapped tart in the freezer, ensuring it's on a flat surface to maintain its shape.

Freezing Individual Slices:

Slice and Wrap:

Cut the tart into individual slices.

Wrap each slice tightly in plastic wrap and then in aluminum foil.

Freeze:

Arrange the wrapped slices in a single layer in the freezer to prevent sticking together.

C. Reheating Instructions for Serving Warm Lemon Tarts

From Refrigeration:

Room Temperature:

If the tart has been refrigerated, allow it to come to room temperature for about 20-30 minutes before serving.

Optional Reheating:

Warm individual slices in a preheated oven at 350°F (175°C) for 5-10 minutes if a slightly warm tart is preferred.

From Freezer:

Thawing:

To thaw a frozen tart, place it in the refrigerator overnight.

Reheating:

Warm in a preheated oven at 350°F (175°C) for 10-15 minutes, checking periodically until it reaches the desired temperature.

Individual Slices:

For frozen slices, unwrap and thaw in the refrigerator or at room temperature, then warm as needed.

By following these storage, freezing, and reheating tips, you can enjoy the freshness and flavors of your lemon tart even days after its initial preparation.

Chapter (8) Lemon Tart as Gifts

A. Packaging Ideas for Gifting Lemon Tarts

Individual Tart Boxes:

Clear Boxes:

Place individual slices of lemon tart in clear plastic or acetate boxes to showcase the delicious layers.

Tie a ribbon around the box for a touch of elegance.

Mini Tart Pans:

Bake mini lemon tarts in disposable tart pans and cover with a decorative lid.

Secure with twine or ribbon and attach a small tag.

Decorative Tins:

Place slices in decorative tins lined with parchment paper.

Wrap the tin with a colorful bow or fabric for a festive look.

B. Personalization Options for a Thoughtful Touch
Custom Tags or Labels:
Name Tags:
Attach small tags with the recipient's name for a personalized touch.
Include a simple message like "Made with Love."
Ingredient List:
Print a small label detailing key ingredients for a charming and informative addition.
This adds a personal connection to the homemade treat.
Special Occasion Tags:
Create tags with greetings for specific occasions, such as birthdays or anniversaries.
C. Printable Recipe Cards for Sharing the Love
Create a Recipe Card:
Design a simple recipe card featuring the lemon tart recipe.
Include a personal note sharing why this dessert is special to you.

Decorative Templates:
Utilize online platforms or graphic design tools to create visually appealing recipe cards.
Include space for personalization and notes.
Attach to Packaging:
Attach the recipe card to the packaging with a decorative clip or ribbon.
This not only provides the recipe but also adds a personal touch to the gift.
Example Recipe Card:
Lemon Tart Recipe
Ingredients:
[List of ingredients]
Instructions:

[Step-by-step instructions]
Tips:
[Additional tips for personalization]
Note:

- This lemon tart is made with love. Enjoy every zesty bite!

By adding these personalization elements, you not only make the gift visually appealing but also create a connection between the giver and the receiver.

Gifting a lemon tart becomes a thoughtful and memorable experience when presented with care and attention to detail.

Chapter (9) Lemon Curd Mastery

A. Homemade Lemon Curd Recipe and Its Role in the Perfect Tart
Homemade Lemon Curd:
Ingredients:

- **3/4 cup fresh lemon juice**
- **Zest of 2 lemons**
- **3/4 cup granulated sugar**
- **3 large eggs**
- **1/2 cup unsalted butter, cubed**

Instructions:

- In a heatproof bowl, whisk together lemon juice, lemon zest, sugar, and eggs.
- Place the bowl over a pot of simmering water (double boiler) without letting the bottom touch the water.
- Whisk continuously until the mixture thickens enough to coat the back of a spoon (about 8-10 minutes).
- Remove from heat and whisk in cubed butter until smooth.
- Strain the curd through a fine-mesh sieve into a clean bowl to remove zest and achieve a silky texture.
- Cover with plastic wrap, ensuring it touches the surface of the curd to prevent a skin from forming.
- Refrigerate until fully chilled before using in the lemon tart.

Role in the Perfect Tart:
Filling Enhancement:
Lemon curd serves as the flavorful and vibrant filling in the lemon tart, intensifying the citrus profile.

Textural Contrast:

Its smooth, velvety consistency provides a pleasing contrast to the tart's buttery crust.

Balancing Sweetness:

The tangy sweetness of lemon curd contributes to the perfect balance of flavors in the tart.

B. Tips for Achieving the Ideal Consistency and Flavor

Fresh Ingredients:

Use fresh lemons for the juice and zest to ensure a robust citrus flavor.

Consistent Whisking:

Whisk continuously during the cooking process to prevent curdling and achieve a smooth texture.

Straining:

Strain the curd to remove any cooked egg bits and achieve a silky consistency.

Butter Incorporation:

Add the cubed butter gradually and whisk until fully incorporated for a rich and velvety curd.

Chilling Time:

Allow the curd to chill thoroughly in the refrigerator to achieve the right consistency for spreading on the tart.

C. Creative Uses for Leftover Lemon Curd in Other Desserts

Lemon Curd Parfait:

Layer lemon curd with whipped cream and crumbled shortbread cookies for a delightful parfait.

Lemon Curd Thumbprint Cookies:

Fill thumbprint cookies with a dollop of lemon curd for a burst of citrus in each bite.

Lemon Curd Cheesecake Bars:

Swirl lemon curd into a cheesecake batter before baking to create tangy and creamy bars.

Lemon Curd Yogurt Bowl:

Mix lemon curd into plain yogurt and top with granola and fresh berries for a refreshing breakfast or snack.

Lemon Curd-Filled Cupcakes:

Fill cupcakes with lemon curd before frosting for a delightful surprise in the center.

Experimenting with leftover lemon curd opens up a world of possibilities, allowing you to infuse its bright and tangy flavor into various desserts beyond the classic tart.

Chapter (10) The Art of Zesting

A. Techniques for Zesting Lemons to Enhance Flavor
Tools Needed:

- Microplane zester or fine grater
- Citrus fruits (lemons, limes, oranges)

Zesting Techniques:
Wash and Dry:
Wash the citrus fruit thoroughly to remove any wax or residue. Dry it completely before zesting.
Hold and Grate:
Hold the lemon firmly and gently glide the Microplane zester or grater over the outer peel.
Use a light, steady hand to avoid bitter pith.
Rotate the Fruit:
Rotate the citrus fruit as you zest to ensure you capture only the outer, flavorful layer.
Collect Zest:
Gather the zest from the Microplane, and be cautious not to press too hard to avoid including bitter white pith.
B. Using Different Citrus Fruits for Unique Zesty Profiles
Zesty Profiles of Different Citrus Fruits:
Lemons:
Bright and zesty with a perfect balance of tartness, ideal for desserts and savory dishes.
Limes:
Zestier and slightly more intense than lemons, lending a vibrant punch to cocktails, marinades, and desserts.
Oranges:

Sweet and aromatic zest, excellent for baking, adding a citrusy twist to glazes, and enhancing salads.

Grapefruits:

Bolder and slightly bitter, grapefruit zest is versatile, working well in both sweet and savory recipes.

Mixing Citrus Zests:

Citrus Medley:

Combine zests from various citrus fruits to create a medley, adding complexity to dishes.

Zesty Blends:

Experiment with different citrus zest blends to tailor flavors to your liking.

C. Infusing Zest into Crusts, Fillings, and Toppings

Crust Infusion:

Lemon Zest Crust:

Add lemon zest to the pie crust (as mentioned in Section II, B) for an extra layer of citrusy goodness.

Filling Enhancement:

Zesty Lemon Filling:

Incorporate lemon zest into the filling of your lemon tart for an intensified citrus flavor (as mentioned in Section III).

Mixed Citrus Medley Filling:

Combine zests from lemons, limes, and oranges for a vibrant and multifaceted citrus filling.

Topping and Garnish:

Zesty Whipped Cream:

Infuse whipped cream with citrus zest for a flavorful topping on the lemon tart.

Candied Citrus Peel:

Candy citrus peels with sugar syrup, creating a sweet and zesty garnish for the tart.

Tips:

Freshness Matters:

Zest citrus fruits just before incorporating them into your recipe for the freshest flavor.

Adjust to Taste:

Experiment with the amount of zest based on personal preference, keeping in mind the intensity of the citrus flavor.

Balance the Flavors:

Ensure the zest complements the overall flavor profile, enhancing without overpowering.

Mastering the art of zesting allows you to unlock the vibrant and aromatic essence of citrus fruits, elevating your lemon tart and other dishes to new heights.

Chapter (11) Perfecting the Crust

A. Exploring Different Crust Textures and Flavors

Classic Shortcrust:

Ingredients:

- 1 1/4 cups all-purpose flour
- 1/2 cup unsalted butter, cold and cubed
- 2 tablespoons granulated sugar
- Pinch of salt
- 2-3 tablespoons ice water

Instructions:

- In a food processor, pulse flour, sugar, and salt.
- Add cold, cubed butter and pulse until the mixture resembles coarse crumbs.
- Gradually add ice water, one tablespoon at a time, and pulse until the dough just comes together.
- Form a disc, wrap in plastic, and refrigerate for at least 30 minutes before rolling out.
- Almond Flour and Coconut Oil Crust (Gluten-Free):

Ingredients:

- 1 1/2 cups almond flour
- 1/4 cup coconut oil, melted
- 2 tablespoons maple syrup or honey
- Pinch of salt

Instructions:

- In a bowl, mix almond flour, melted coconut oil, maple syrup, and a pinch of salt until combined.

- Press the mixture into a tart pan and chill in the refrigerator for 15-20 minutes.
- Oat and Walnut Crust (Nut-Based):

Ingredients:

- **1 cup old-fashioned oats**
- **1/2 cup walnuts**
- **2 tablespoons maple syrup**
- **2 tablespoons coconut oil, melted**

Instructions:

- Blend oats and walnuts in a food processor until finely ground.
- Add maple syrup and melted coconut oil, pulsing until the mixture holds together.
- Press into a tart pan and refrigerate for 15-20 minutes before baking.
- Blind Baking Tips for a Crisp and Flaky Foundation

Blind Baking Steps:
Preheat:

- Preheat your oven to 375°F (190°C).

Prepare the Crust:

- Roll out the crust and press it into the tart pan.

Dock the Crust:

- Prick the bottom of the crust with a fork to prevent it from puffing up during baking.

Use Pie Weights:

- Line the crust with parchment paper and fill it with pie weights or dried beans.

Bake:

- Bake in the preheated oven for 15-20 minutes or until the edges are set.

Remove Weights:

- Carefully remove the parchment paper and weights, then return the crust to the oven to bake for an additional 5-10 minutes or until golden brown.

C. Gluten-Free and Nut-Based Crust Alternatives
Gluten-Free Almond Flour Crust (as mentioned in Section V, A):
Ingredients:

- **1 1/2 cups almond flour**
- **1/4 cup coconut flour**
- **1/4 cup melted coconut oil or dairy-free butter**
- **2 tablespoons maple syrup or agave nectar**
- **Pinch of salt**

Instructions:

- Mix almond flour, coconut flour, melted coconut oil, maple syrup, and a pinch of salt.
- Press into a tart pan and bake according to the tart recipe instructions.
- Nut-Based Oat and Walnut Crust (as mentioned above):

Ingredients:

- 1 cup old-fashioned oats
- 1/2 cup walnuts
- 2 tablespoons maple syrup
- 2 tablespoons coconut oil, melted

Instructions:

- Blend oats and walnuts, then mix with maple syrup and melted coconut oil.
- Press into a tart pan and refrigerate before baking.
- Experiment with these crust variations to find the texture and flavor that best complements your lemon tart. Whether you prefer a classic shortcrust, a gluten-free almond flour crust, or a nut-based option, the crust sets the foundation for a delicious and perfect tart.

Chapter (12) Showstopper Lemon Tart Decorations

A. Advanced Garnishing Techniques for a Stunning Presentation

Piping Techniques:

Whipped Cream Rosettes:

Use a piping bag with a star tip to create intricate rosettes along the edges of the tart.

Chocolate Ganache Drizzle:

Melt dark or white chocolate and drizzle it over the tart using a piping bag for an elegant touch.

Fruit Arrangements:

Citrus Slices Spiral:

Arrange thin slices of lemon, lime, and orange in a spiral pattern on top of the tart for a visually striking effect.

Berries Mosaic:

Create a mosaic pattern using a variety of fresh berries like strawberries, blueberries, and raspberries.

B. Edible Flowers, Candied Citrus, and Chocolate Accents

Edible Flowers:

Pansies or Violets:

Place whole pansies or violets on top of the tart for a delicate and colorful floral touch.

Candied Flower Petals:

Candied flower petals, such as rose or lavender, add both sweetness and beauty to the presentation.

Candied Citrus:

Candied Lemon Slices:

Thinly slice lemons, dip them in a sugar syrup, and let them dry. Arrange these candied slices on top of the tart for a sweet and tangy decoration.

Candied Citrus Peel Strips:

Create thin strips of candied lemon or orange peel and arrange them in artistic patterns on the tart.

Chocolate Accents:

Chocolate Shards:

Make chocolate shards by melting chocolate, spreading it thin on parchment paper, and breaking it into geometric shapes to decorate the tart.

Chocolate Curls:

Use a vegetable peeler to create delicate chocolate curls, arranging them in swirls or clusters on the tart.

C. Turning Your Lemon Tart into a Work of Art

Geometric Designs:

Lemon Zest Patterns:

Use finely grated lemon zest to create intricate patterns or even write personalized messages on the surface of the tart.

Chocolate Artwork:

Melted chocolate can be used to paint artistic designs on the tart, from abstract patterns to detailed illustrations.

Layered Decorative Elements:

Multi-Layered Garnishes:

Combine different decorative elements, such as edible flowers, chocolate shards, and citrus slices, for a multi-layered and visually stunning presentation.

Elevated Presentation:

Place the tart on a tiered cake stand to add height and drama to the overall presentation.

Remember, the key to turning your lemon tart into a showstopper is creativity and attention to detail. Experiment with different combinations of garnishes, textures, and colors to create a visually striking masterpiece that not only delights the taste buds but also captivates the eyes.

Chapter (13) Lemon Tart Pairing Guide

A. Matching Lemon Tart with Wines, Spirits, and Non-Alcoholic Beverages

Wine Pairing:

Sweet White Wine:

Pair with a late-harvest Riesling or a Moscato for a delightful contrast to the tartness of the lemon.

Sparkling Wine:

Champagne or prosecco complements the citrusy notes, while the bubbles cleanse the palate.

Dessert Wine:

Opt for a sweet Sauternes or a botrytis-affected wine for a rich and luxurious pairing.

Spirits:

Limoncello:

This lemon-flavored liqueur serves as both a delightful accompaniment and a digestif.

Gin and Tonic:

The botanicals in gin and the effervescence of tonic water provide a refreshing contrast.

Citrus-Infused Vodka:

Serve lemon tart with a citrus-infused vodka cocktail for a harmonious pairing.

Non-Alcoholic Beverages:

Iced Tea:

A cold and slightly sweetened black or green tea complements the tartness of the lemon.

Lemonade with a Twist:

Enhance traditional lemonade with additional citrus fruits or herbs for a refreshing non-alcoholic option.

B. Complementary Flavors in Cheeses and Ice Creams

Cheeses:

Mascarpone:

The creamy and mild sweetness of mascarpone balances the tartness of the lemon tart.

Goat Cheese:

A tangy goat cheese adds a savory element that contrasts with the sweet and citrusy flavors.

Brie or Camembert:

Creamy, soft cheeses with a mild flavor profile complement the richness of the lemon tart.

Ice Creams:

Lemon Sorbet:

A scoop of lemon sorbet intensifies the citrus experience and refreshes the palate.

Vanilla Bean Ice Cream:

The classic vanilla flavor provides a neutral base that enhances the lemony notes.

Basil or Mint Infused Ice Cream:

Herb-infused ice creams add a unique and herbal dimension to the dessert.

C. Creating a Balanced Dessert Spread for Entertaining

Dessert Spread Ideas:

Chocolate Desserts:

Include a selection of chocolate desserts, such as brownies or chocolate mousse, for those who prefer a richer flavor profile.

Fruit-Centric Desserts:

Offer a variety of fruit-based desserts like berry tarts or fruit salads to balance the sweetness.

Nutty Treats:

Include nut-based desserts like almond cake or pistachio cookies for added texture and variety.

Coffee or Tea Bar:

Provide a selection of coffee and tea options to complement the diverse flavors of the desserts.

Assorted Mini Desserts:

Serve an assortment of mini desserts to allow guests to sample different flavors without committing to a full serving.

Remember to consider the preferences of your guests when planning the dessert spread. A well-curated selection ensures that everyone can find a delightful treat to enjoy alongside the exquisite lemon tart.

Chapter (14) Mini Lemon Tartlets

A. Recipe for Bite-Sized Lemon Tartlets
Mini Lemon Tartlet Shells:
Ingredients:

- 1 cup all-purpose flour
- 1/4 cup powdered sugar
- 1/2 cup unsalted butter, cold and cubed

Instructions:

- Preheat the oven to 350°F (175°C).
- In a food processor, combine flour, powdered sugar, and cold butter. Pulse until the mixture resembles fine crumbs.
- Press the mixture into mini tartlet pans, ensuring an even layer on the bottom and sides.
- Prick the bottoms with a fork and chill in the refrigerator for 15 minutes.
- Bake for 12-15 minutes or until the edges are golden. Let the tartlet shells cool completely.

Mini Lemon Tartlet Filling:
Ingredients:

- 1/2 cup lemon curd (homemade or store-bought)

Instructions:

- Fill each cooled tartlet shell with approximately 1 teaspoon of lemon curd.
- Smooth the surface of the lemon curd in each tartlet.

B. Perfect for Parties and Gatherings
Advantages of Mini Lemon Tartlets:
Easy Serving:
Mini tartlets are individually portioned, making them convenient for guests to grab and enjoy.
Variety of Flavors:
Prepare a variety of mini tartlets with different fillings to cater to various taste preferences.
Visual Appeal:
The bite-sized nature of these tartlets creates an attractive display, adding to the overall aesthetic of your dessert spread.
Versatile Presentation:
Arrange the mini tartlets on tiered trays or platters for an elegant and organized presentation at parties.

C. Variations on Fillings and Crusts for Mini Delights
Filling Variations:
Berry Medley Tartlets:
Top the lemon curd with a mix of fresh berries such as raspberries, blueberries, and strawberries.
Chocolate Ganache Mini Tarts:
Spread a thin layer of chocolate ganache at the bottom of the tartlet shells before adding the lemon curd.
Lemon Lavender Tartlets:
Infuse the lemon curd with a touch of lavender essence for a unique and aromatic twist.
Crust Variations:
Almond Mini Tartlets (Gluten-Free):
Substitute almond flour for part or all of the all-purpose flour in the crust recipe.
Graham Cracker Crust Mini Tarts:

Mix crushed graham crackers with melted butter to create a simple and delicious crust alternative.

Coconut Shortcrust Mini Tartlets:

Add shredded coconut to the crust mixture for a tropical flavor that complements the lemon filling.

Experiment with different combinations to create a diverse array of mini lemon tartlets that cater to various taste preferences and dietary needs. The small size allows for creativity and personalization in crafting the perfect bite-sized treats for your gatherings.

Chapter (15) Savory Lemon Tarts

A. Exploring the Savory Side of Lemon-Infused Tarts

Savory Lemon Tart Concept:

Savory lemon tarts provide a delightful twist by balancing the bright acidity of lemons with savory and umami flavors. The combination of a buttery crust and zesty lemon filling creates a versatile canvas for savory ingredients.

B. Incorporating Herbs, Cheeses, and Vegetables

Savory Lemon Tart Filling:

Ingredients:

- 1 cup ricotta cheese
- 1/2 cup grated Parmesan cheese
- Zest of 1 lemon
- 2 tablespoons fresh lemon juice
- 2 tablespoons chopped fresh herbs (such as thyme, rosemary, or chives)
- Salt and pepper to taste

Instructions:

- In a bowl, mix ricotta, Parmesan, lemon zest, lemon juice, and fresh herbs until well combined.
- Season with salt and pepper to taste.
- Use this savory filling as the base for your savory lemon tart.

Vegetable Toppings:
Roasted Cherry Tomatoes:

Toss cherry tomatoes with olive oil, salt, and pepper, then roast until slightly caramelized. Top the tart with these flavorful tomatoes.

Caramelized Onions:

Slowly caramelize onions in butter until golden brown and sweet. Spread a layer over the savory filling.

Sautéed Spinach or Kale:

Sauté leafy greens in olive oil and garlic, then add them as a vibrant and nutritious topping.

Cheese Options:

Goat Cheese:

Crumbled goat cheese adds tanginess and creaminess to the savory lemon tart.

Feta Cheese:

Incorporate crumbled feta for a briny and salty flavor that pairs well with the lemon.

Gruyère or Swiss Cheese:

Use shredded Gruyère or Swiss cheese for a rich and nutty element in the filling.

C. Ideal for Brunches and Light Lunches

Serving Suggestions:

Brunch Buffet:

Cut savory lemon tarts into smaller portions for a brunch buffet, allowing guests to enjoy a variety of flavors.

Light Lunch Entrée:

Serve larger slices of savory lemon tart as a light and satisfying lunch option alongside a crisp salad.

Picnic Delight:

Pack individual portions of savory lemon tart for a flavorful addition to a picnic spread.

Beverage Pairing:

Iced Tea or Lemonade:

The tartness of the lemon in the savory tart pairs well with refreshing iced tea or lemonade.

White Wine:

A crisp and light white wine, such as Sauvignon Blanc or Pinot Grigio, complements the savory and citrusy notes.

Herbal Infusions:

Consider serving herbal infusions like mint or basil tea for a refreshing and aromatic pairing.

Savory lemon tarts provide a sophisticated and unexpected twist on traditional lemon desserts. By incorporating herbs, cheeses, and vegetables, you can create a versatile dish ideal for various occasions, from brunch gatherings to light lunches.

Chapter (16) Lemon Tart Inspired Breakfast

A. Incorporating Lemon Tart Flavors into Breakfast Recipes

Lemon Tart Breakfast Concept:

Bring the zesty and vibrant flavors of lemon tarts to your breakfast table by infusing classic breakfast items with citrus goodness. From pancakes to muffins, these recipes will add a delightful twist to your morning routine.

B. Lemon-Infused Pancakes, Waffles, and Muffins

Lemon Pancakes:

Ingredients:

- 1 cup all-purpose flour
- 1 tablespoon sugar
- 1 teaspoon baking powder
- 1/2 teaspoon baking soda
- 1/4 teaspoon salt
- 3/4 cup buttermilk
- 1 large egg
- 2 tablespoons unsalted butter, melted
- Zest of 1 lemon
- 2 tablespoons fresh lemon juice

Instructions:

- In a bowl, whisk together flour, sugar, baking powder, baking soda, and salt.
- In a separate bowl, whisk together buttermilk, egg, melted butter, lemon zest, and lemon juice.
- Pour the wet ingredients into the dry ingredients and gently

mix until just combined.

- Heat a griddle or non-stick pan over medium heat. Pour 1/4 cup batter for each pancake.
- Cook until bubbles form on the surface, then flip and cook until golden brown.
- Serve with a drizzle of maple syrup and additional lemon zest.

Lemon Waffles:
Ingredients:

- **1 3/4 cups all-purpose flour**
- **2 tablespoons sugar**
- **1 tablespoon baking powder**
- **1/2 teaspoon salt**
- **1 1/2 cups milk**
- **1/3 cup vegetable oil**
- **2 large eggs**
- **Zest of 2 lemons**
- **1/4 cup fresh lemon juice**

Instructions:

- Preheat your waffle iron according to the manufacturer's instructions.
- In a bowl, whisk together flour, sugar, baking powder, and salt.
- In another bowl, whisk together milk, vegetable oil, eggs, lemon zest, and lemon juice.
- Add the wet ingredients to the dry ingredients and stir until just combined.
- Pour the batter onto the preheated waffle iron and cook according to the manufacturer's instructions.
- Serve the waffles with a dollop of whipped cream and a sprinkle of lemon zest.

Lemon Poppy Seed Muffins:
Ingredients:

- **2 cups all-purpose flour**
- **1 cup granulated sugar**
- **1 tablespoon poppy seeds**
- **1 tablespoon baking powder**
- **1/2 teaspoon baking soda**
- **1/4 teaspoon salt**
- **1 cup buttermilk**
- **1/2 cup unsalted butter, melted**
- **2 large eggs**
- **Zest of 2 lemons**
- **1/4 cup fresh lemon juice**

Instructions:

- Preheat the oven to 375°F (190°C) and line a muffin tin with paper liners.
- In a large bowl, whisk together flour, sugar, poppy seeds, baking powder, baking soda, and salt.
- In another bowl, whisk together buttermilk, melted butter, eggs, lemon zest, and lemon juice.
- Add the wet ingredients to the dry ingredients and stir until just combined.
- Divide the batter evenly among the muffin cups.
- Bake for 18-20 minutes or until a toothpick inserted into the center comes out clean.
- Cool the muffins in the tin for 5 minutes before transferring them to a wire rack to cool completely.

C. Starting the Day with a Burst of Citrus Goodness
Breakfast Pairing Ideas:

Greek Yogurt Parfait:

Layer lemon-infused pancakes or waffles with Greek yogurt and fresh berries for a vibrant and protein-packed breakfast.

Citrus Salad:

Toss together a citrus salad with segments of oranges, grapefruits, and lemon zest to accompany your lemon poppy seed muffins.

Lemon Ricotta Toast:

Spread a mixture of ricotta cheese and lemon zest on whole-grain toast for a simple and satisfying breakfast.

Lemon-Infused Smoothie:

Blend together frozen berries, banana, yogurt, and a splash of lemon juice for a refreshing and nutritious smoothie.

By infusing your breakfast with the flavors of lemon tarts, you can elevate your morning routine and start the day with a burst of citrus goodness. Whether you opt for lemon pancakes, waffles, muffins, or creative breakfast pairings, these recipes bring a touch of sweetness and brightness to the most important meal of the day.

Chapter (17) Healthier Lemon Tart Options

A. Low-Sugar and Reduced-Fat Variations

Low-Sugar Lemon Tart Filling:

Ingredients:

- 1 cup fresh lemon juice
- Zest of 2 lemons
- 3/4 cup natural sweetener (such as stevia, erythritol, or monk fruit)
- 4 large eggs
- 1/2 cup Greek yogurt (reduced-fat or fat-free)

Instructions:

- In a bowl, whisk together lemon juice, lemon zest, natural sweetener, and eggs.
- Gently fold in Greek yogurt until smooth.
- Use this reduced-sugar and reduced-fat filling in your favorite lemon tart recipe.

Alternative Sweeteners:

Stevia:

Use liquid or powdered stevia as a sugar substitute. Adjust the amount to your desired level of sweetness.

Erythritol or Monk Fruit:

These natural sweeteners can be used as a 1:1 substitute for sugar in most recipes.

Reduced-Fat Crust:

Ingredients:

- 1 cup almond flour
- 1/4 cup coconut flour
- 2 tablespoons melted coconut oil (or another healthy oil)
- 1 tablespoon natural sweetener
- Pinch of salt

Instructions:

- Mix almond flour, coconut flour, melted coconut oil, natural sweetener, and a pinch of salt.
- Press the mixture into the tart pan and bake according to your recipe's instructions.

B. Nutritional Tips for a Guilt-Free Indulgence
Portion Control:
Mini Tartlets:
Opt for mini tartlets to naturally limit portion sizes while still enjoying the delightful flavors.

Thin Slices:
Cut the lemon tart into thin slices, allowing for a satisfying taste without excessive calories.
Nutrient-Rich Ingredients:
Whole Wheat Flour:
Choose whole wheat flour for the crust to add fiber and nutrients.
Greek Yogurt:
Replace some or all of the cream with Greek yogurt for a protein boost with less fat.
Almond Flour:

Incorporate almond flour into the crust for a nutrient-dense alternative to traditional flour.

C. Using Natural Sweeteners and Alternative Crusts

Natural Sweetener Blend:

Maple Syrup and Agave Nectar:

Create a natural sweetener blend using equal parts of maple syrup and agave nectar for a richer flavor.

Honey:

Use raw honey for its natural sweetness and added health benefits.

Alternative Crust Options:

Oat and Nut Crust:

Combine ground oats and finely chopped nuts with a bit of coconut oil for a wholesome crust.

Coconut Flour Crust:

Create a gluten-free crust using coconut flour, coconut oil, and a natural sweetener.

Quinoa Crust:

Incorporate cooked quinoa into your crust for added protein and a unique texture.

Fresh Fruit Topping:

Berries and Citrus Slices:

Top your lemon tart with fresh berries and citrus slices for added vitamins and antioxidants.

Kiwi and Mango:

Add slices of kiwi and mango for a tropical twist that enhances both flavor and nutrition.

Additional Tips:

Reduce Serving Size:

Enjoy a smaller serving of lemon tart, savoring each bite.

Enhance with Herbs:

Infuse the filling with a touch of fresh herbs like mint or basil for added depth of flavor.

By making thoughtful ingredient substitutions and being mindful of portion sizes, you can create a healthier version of the classic lemon tart without compromising on taste. These alternatives allow for guilt-free indulgence, making it easier to enjoy this delightful dessert as part of a balanced and nutritious lifestyle.

Chapter (18) Global Lemon Tart Influences

A. Exploring Lemon Tart Variations from Different Cultures

French Tarte au Citron:

Features:

Buttery and flaky pastry crust.

Tangy lemon curd filling made with fresh lemon juice and zest.

Often served with a dusting of powdered sugar or a thin layer of meringue.

Italian Crostata al Limone:

Features:

Shortcrust pastry with a hint of sweetness.

Lemon custard filling made with eggs, sugar, and fresh lemon juice.

Garnished with candied lemon peel or a lemon glaze.

Moroccan Meskouta:

Features:

Moist and dense lemon cake.

Incorporates semolina or almond flour for a unique texture.

Often flavored with orange blossom water or rose water.

American Lemon Chess Pie:

Features:

Simple pie crust with a custard-like filling.

Lemon chess pie filling made with sugar, butter, eggs, and lemon juice.

May have a crackly sugar crust on top.

B. Traditional Recipes and Unique Twists

British Lemon Drizzle Cake:

Features:

Light and fluffy sponge cake.

Drizzled with a sweet and tangy lemon syrup.

Can be served with a dollop of clotted cream or a dusting of icing sugar.

Japanese Yuzu Tart:

Features:

Yuzu-flavored tart with a buttery crust.

Yuzu, a Japanese citrus fruit, adds a unique and aromatic flavor.

Sometimes topped with a layer of yuzu-flavored jelly for extra brightness.

Indian Nimbu Ka Meetha:

Features:

Sweet and tangy lemon dessert popular in Indian cuisine.

May include ingredients like condensed milk, khoya (reduced milk), and ground nuts.

Garnished with chopped pistachios or almonds.

Australian Lemon Myrtle Pie:

Features:

Lemon myrtle, a native Australian plant, infuses the pie with a lemony and herbal flavor.

Graham cracker or biscuit crust.

Often served with a dollop of whipped cream or a scoop of vanilla ice cream.

C. Adapting International Flavors to Your Own Lemon Tart Creations

Fusion Flavors:

Mango and Coconut Fusion:

Combine the tropical flavors of mango and coconut in your lemon tart for a refreshing and exotic twist.

Lemon Matcha Tart:

Infuse your lemon tart with matcha powder for a subtle earthy flavor and vibrant green color.

Spices and Herbs:

Lemon Cardamom Tart:

Add ground cardamom to your lemon tart for a warm and aromatic touch.

Lemon Basil Tart:

Incorporate fresh basil into the filling for a unique herbal note.

Alcohol-Infused:

Limoncello-Infused Tart:

Replace some of the lemon juice with limoncello for an Italian-inspired twist.

Gin and Tonic Lemon Tart:

Infuse the lemon tart filling with the botanicals of gin and a hint of tonic water for a sophisticated flavor profile.

Nut-Based Crusts:
Macadamia Nut Crust:
Substitute traditional crust with a macadamia nut crust for a buttery and rich base.

Pistachio and Almond Crust:
Combine ground pistachios and almonds for a nutty and flavorful crust.

Explore the diverse lemon tart variations from around the world, draw inspiration from different culinary traditions, and experiment with unique flavor combinations to create your own global-inspired lemon tart creations. Whether you prefer the classic French Tarte au Citron or want to infuse Japanese yuzu flavors into your tart, the possibilities are endless for creating a lemony masterpiece that reflects your culinary creativity.

Chapter (19) Lemon Tart Challenges

A. Participating in Lemon Tart Baking Challenges
Online Baking Challenges:
Social Media Challenges:
Join baking challenges on platforms like Instagram or TikTok, where participants share their lemon tart creations using a specific hashtag.
Baking Competitions:
Look for virtual baking competitions or local events that feature lemon tart challenges. Participating can be a fun way to showcase your skills.

B. Engaging with the Baking Community for Tips and Inspiration
Online Baking Communities:
Baking Forums:
Join online baking forums or communities to connect with other enthusiasts. Share your lemon tart experiences and learn from others.
Social Media Groups:
Participate in baking groups on Facebook or other social media platforms. Exchange tips, troubleshoot issues, and find inspiration for your lemon tart endeavors.
Collaboration with Fellow Bakers:
Virtual Baking Workshops:
Attend virtual baking workshops or organize one with fellow bakers. Discuss techniques, share recipes, and collectively troubleshoot challenges.
Baking Challenges with Friends:
Challenge your friends or baking buddies to a friendly lemon tart bake-off. Exchange recipes and taste each other's creations for valuable feedback.

C. Overcoming Common Hurdles for a Perfect Lemon Tart Outcome

Common Lemon Tart Challenges and Solutions:

Soggy Crust:

Solution: Blind bake the crust before adding the filling. Brush the crust with a thin layer of beaten egg to create a moisture barrier.

Curdling in Filling:

Solution: Gradually add lemon juice to the egg mixture and ensure it's well incorporated. Use room temperature ingredients to prevent curdling.

Cracking on the Surface:

Solution: Bake the tart at a lower temperature and avoid overmixing the filling. Allow the tart to cool gradually to minimize cracks.

Uneven Filling Settling:

Solution: Tap the tart pan gently on the counter to remove air bubbles before baking. Use a water bath for a more even and gradual bake.

Browning Too Quickly:

Solution: Cover the tart with foil halfway through baking or adjust the oven temperature. Keep a close eye on the tart to prevent excessive browning.

Difficulty Removing from Pan:

Solution: Ensure the tart has cooled sufficiently before removing it from the pan. If using a removable-bottom pan, gently release the sides before transferring.

Overly Tart or Sweet Filling:

Solution: Adjust the balance of sweetness and tartness by gradually adding more sugar or lemon juice, according to your taste preference.

Seeking Feedback:
Tasting Panels:
Invite friends, family, or neighbors to taste-test your lemon tart. Gather feedback on flavor, texture, and overall appeal.
Online Feedback:
Share pictures and descriptions of your lemon tart on baking forums or social media groups. Ask for constructive feedback and suggestions for improvement.

Overcoming challenges in the pursuit of the perfect lemon tart is part of the baking journey. Engaging with the baking community, participating in challenges, and seeking feedback will not only enhance your skills but also make the process more enjoyable. Every hurdle is an opportunity to learn and refine your lemon tart-making prowess.

Chapter (20) Lemon Tart Catering

A. Scaling Up the Recipe for Large Gatherings
Large-Batch Lemon Tart Filling:
Ingredients:

- **4 cups fresh lemon juice**
- **Zest of 8 lemons**
- **3 cups granulated sugar**
- **16 large eggs**
- **2 cups Greek yogurt**

Instructions:

- Whisk together lemon juice, lemon zest, sugar, eggs, and Greek yogurt in a large mixing bowl until well combined.
- Adjust sweetness and tartness according to taste.
- Use this filling in batches for multiple tart shells.

Crust Scaling Tips:
Use Commercial Sheet Pans:
Consider using commercial-sized sheet pans for baking multiple tart crusts simultaneously.
Pre-Baked Tart Shells:
Pre-bake tart shells ahead of time and freeze them. Thaw and fill when needed for efficient preparation.
B. Tips for Transporting and Serving Lemon Tarts at Events
Transporting:
Secure Packaging:
Place individual or stacked tart boxes in sturdy containers to prevent shifting during transport.
Chilled Transportation:

Transport lemon tarts in a cooler with ice packs to maintain their freshness.

Serving at Events:

Temperature Considerations:

If possible, store lemon tarts in a refrigerated display or serve them on a dessert table with cooling elements.

Mini Tartlets for Events:

Consider preparing mini lemon tartlets for easier handling and serving at events.

Serve with Style:

Use elegant platters, tiered stands, or dessert trays to showcase the lemon tarts attractively.

C. Creating a Dessert Table Centerpiece

Visual Presentation:

Tiered Dessert Stand:

Arrange lemon tarts on a tiered dessert stand to create a visually appealing centerpiece.

Decorative Elements:

Garnish the dessert table with fresh flowers, citrus slices, or greenery for a decorative touch.

Flavor Variation:

Assorted Lemon Tart Varieties:

Showcase different lemon tart variations, such as lavender-infused or citrus medley tartlets, for variety.

Accompanying Elements:

Include complementary items like whipped cream, berries, and mint for guests to customize their servings.

Personalized Touch:

Printed Dessert Labels:

Create small labels with the names and brief descriptions of each lemon tart variety.

Customized Packaging:

Personalize packaging with labels, ribbons, or tags to add a special touch for guests.

Interactive Dessert Stations:

DIY Lemon Tart Station:

Set up a DIY lemon tart station where guests can assemble their own tart with various toppings and garnishes.

Chef's Live Demo:

Consider having a live demonstration where a chef prepares and garnishes lemon tarts, engaging guests in the culinary experience.

By scaling up the recipe, optimizing transportation logistics, and creating an enticing dessert table presentation, you can successfully cater lemon tarts for large gatherings. Whether it's a wedding, corporate event, or celebration, these tips ensure a delightful and visually stunning experience for guests.

❖ Conclusion

A. Recap of Key Tips and Techniques

Fresh Ingredients Matter:

Choose high-quality, fresh lemons for the best flavor in your lemon tart.

Perfecting the Crust:

Pay attention to crust texture, try different variations, and master blind baking for a crisp and flaky foundation.

Balancing Sweetness and Tartness:

Experiment with sugar levels and lemon juice to achieve the perfect balance in the filling.

Variety is the Spice of Life:

Explore variations like Citrus Medley, Lavender, and Toasted Coconut to add excitement to the classic lemon tart.

Dietary Accommodations:

Consider gluten-free and vegan options using almond flour, alternative sweeteners, and dairy-free alternatives.

Garnishes and Presentation:

Elevate the visual appeal with whipped cream, berries, and creative plating for special occasions.

Lemon-Inspired Beverages:

Pair your lemon tart with refreshing lemonade, cocktails, or teas for a complete experience.

Storage and Freezing Tips:

Follow proper storage techniques and freezing guidelines for make-ahead convenience.

Gift-Worthy Treats:

Package your lemon tarts creatively, personalize them, and share the love with printable recipe cards.

Further Explorations:

Experiment with lemon curd, zesting techniques, unique crusts, and advanced garnishing for an elevated experience.

B. Encouragement for Readers to Explore and Experiment with Lemon Tart Variations

Embark on a culinary adventure with your lemon tarts. Don't be afraid to push boundaries and infuse your unique personality into each creation. Try unexpected flavor combinations, explore different crust textures, and let your creativity shine. The joy of baking is not just in the result but in the journey of experimentation and discovery.

C. Closing Thoughts on the Joy of Creating and Sharing This Delightful Dessert

The joy of creating a lemon tart extends beyond the kitchen. It's about sharing moments of sweetness and delight with those around you. Whether it's a quiet evening indulging in a slice, a festive gathering, or a thoughtful gift to a friend, the joy lies in the shared experience. The tangy aroma, the burst of citrus on the palate, and the smiles it brings—these are the true rewards of crafting a perfect lemon tart. May your culinary endeavors continue to bring joy and connection to your life and those you share it with. Happy baking!